The Quotation Bank

Animal Farm

George Orwell

Introduction

Quotations

Revision and Essay Planning

Whilst you may have read the novel, watched a film adaptation, understood the plot and have a strong grasp of context, the vast majority of marks awarded in your GCSE are for the ability to write a focused essay, full of quotations, and most importantly, quotations that you then analyse.

I think we all agree it is **analysis** that is the tricky part – and that is why we are here to help!

The Quotation Bank takes 25 of the most important quotations from the text, interprets them, analyses them, highlights literary techniques Orwell has used, puts them in context, and suggests which quotations you might use in which essays.

At the end of **The Quotation Bank** we have put together a sample answer, essay plans and great revision exercises to help you prepare for your exam. We have also included a detailed glossary to make sure you completely understand what certain literary terms actually mean!

All GCSE Exam Boards mark your exams using the same Assessment Objectives (AOs) – around 80% of your mark across the English Literature GCSE will be awarded for A01 and A02.

A01	Read, understand and respond to texts. Students should be able to: • Maintain a critical style and develop an ***informed personal response*** • Use textual references, ***including quotations***, to support and illustrate ***interpretations***.
A02	Analyse the ***Language, Form and Structure*** used by a writer to ***create meanings and effects***, using ***relevant subject terminology*** where appropriate.

Basically, **AO1** is the ability to answer the question set, showing a good knowledge of the text, and using quotations to back up ideas and interpretations.

AO2 is the ability to analyse these quotations, as well as the literary techniques the writer uses, and to show you understand the effect of these on the reader.

We will also highlight elements of **AO3** – the context in which the novel is set.

The Quotation Bank is designed to make sure that every point you make in an essay clearly fulfils the Assessment Objectives an examiner will be using when marking your work.

Every quotation comes with the following detailed material:

Interpretation: The interpretation of each quotation allows you to fulfil **AO1**, responding to the text and giving an informed personal response.

Techniques: Using subject-specific terminology correctly (in this case, the literary devices used by Orwell) is a key part of **AO2**.

Analysis: We have provided as much analysis (**AO2**) as possible. It is a great idea to analyse the quotation in detail – you need to do more than just say what it means, but also what effect the language, form and structure has on the reader.

Use in essays on… Your answer needs to be focused to fulfil **AO1**. This section helps you choose relevant quotations and link them together for a stronger essay.

Many students spend time learning quotations by heart.

This is an excellent idea, but they often forget what they are meant to do with those quotations once they get into the exam!

By using **The Quotation Bank**, not only will you have a huge number of quotations to use in your essays, you will also have ideas on what to say about them, how to analyse them, how to link them together, and what questions to use them for.

For GCSE essay questions, these quotations can form the basis of your answer, making sure every point comes **directly from the text (AO1)** and allowing you to **analyse language, form and structure (AO2)**. We also highlight where you can easily and effectively include **context (AO3)**.

For GCSE questions that give you an extract to analyse, the quotations in **The Quotation Bank** are excellent not only for revising the skills of **analysis (AO2)**, but also for showing **wider understanding of the text (AO1)**.

> **"Now, comrades, what is the nature of this life of ours? Let us face it, our lives are miserable, laborious and short."**

Interpretation: From the outset of the novel the reader is introduced to the lack of hope present in the animals' lives and the oppressive environment in which they live.

Techniques: Pronouns; Tri-colon (or list of three).

Analysis:

- The singular "life" alongside the pronoun "ours" implies Major believes all animals are one united being, and most importantly, all equal.
- The noun "comrades" and pronouns "us" and "ours" have associations of togetherness and unity, but language changes as the novel progresses and they become terms used to manipulate and confuse the animals.
- The tri-colon stresses the animals' suffering is physical ("laborious"), mental ("miserable") and life-limiting ("short").

Use in essays on… Hope; Class; Power; Truth.

Chapter One:

"Is it not crystal clear, then, comrades, that all the evils of this life of ours spring from the tyranny of human beings?"

Interpretation: Major's dream is not one of rebellion and violence, but instead a desire to see all animals treated fairly and equally; it is humans who cause suffering.

Techniques: Rhetorical Question; Alliteration; Language.

Analysis:

- Major's rhetorical question is a powerful technique in speech making, used to convince the animals that what he says is fact – however, later in the novel Squealer and Napoleon use the same technique to control the animals.
- The alliteration in "crystal clear" emphasises the clarity and purity of Major's vision; this is juxtaposed with the corrupt ideas and leadership of Napoleon.
- "Evils" and "tyranny" convey the sheer brutality of farm life under Jones – "spring" suggests the farmers get an active enjoyment from this behaviour.

Use in essays on…Power; Violence; Corruption; Truth.

Chapter Two:
"The harness room at the end of the stables was broken open; the bits, the nose-rings, the dog-chains, the cruel knives with which Mr Jones had been used to castrate the pigs and lambs, were all flung down the well."

Interpretation: Whilst farmers (and the reader) may see the list of equipment as necessary to the safe running of a farm, to animals they are symbols of violent control.

Techniques: Listing; Personification.

Analysis:

- "Broken open" and "flung down" are active, dynamic images – they both suggest an explosion of physical freedom and release for the animals.
- The lengthy list stresses the range of tools and implements used by humans to inflict pain and oppress the animals. "Bits", "nose-rings" and "chains" depict painful physical restriction.
- The "knives" are personified as "cruel", and, alongside "castrate", suggest an even darker element of evil control than Major depicted.

Use in essays on… Violence; Power; Corruption.

Chapter Two:
"They rolled in the dew, they cropped mouthfuls of the sweet summer grass, they kicked up clods of the black earth and snuffed its rich scent."

Interpretation: The beautiful, natural environment of the farm, alongside the abundant riches it provides, suggests Major's utopian dream can be easily achieved.

Techniques: Sibilance; Tone; Imagery.

Analysis:

- The natural imagery of "dew", "summer grass" and "black earth" depicts nature as it should be enjoyed, not as it was under the tyranny of Jones.
- The sibilance of "sweet summer grass" and "snuffed its rich scent" creates an overwhelmingly joyous, pleasurable experience for all to engage with.
- All animals revel in the vast sensual wonders of the farm – the touch ("rolled" and "kicked"), taste ("mouthfuls" and "sweet") and smells ("rich scent") convey their complete engagement with its delights.

Use in essays on… Hope; Truth; Class.

"These seven commandments would now be inscribed on the wall; they would form an unalterable law by which all the animals on Animal Farm must live for ever after."

Interpretation: Animalism has been achieved – Major's vision now has a formal written code to follow so that all animals can be liberated, free, and most importantly, equal.

Techniques: Tone; Allusion.

Analysis:

- "Commandments" has deeply biblical allusions, implying the laws have a religious truth, and all must follow them.
- "Unalterable", "all", "must" and "for ever" are words meant to convey liberation, but there is a clear tone of restriction in the language used.
- The language surrounding the commandments implies an unbreakable, eternal way of living that will bring equality. However, the ignorance of many animals means these commandments can be corrupted to fit the pigs' desires.

Use in essays on…Power; Corruption; Ignorance; Responsibility; Truth; Class.

Chapter Three:
   "Every mouthful of food was an acute positive pleasure, now that it was truly their own food, produced by themselves and for themselves, not doled out to them by a grudging master."

Interpretation: Major claimed "Man" was the "root cause of hunger and overwork". Here the reader sees animals living the harmonious, plentiful life of equality he predicted.

Techniques: Alliteration; Repetition; Foreshadowing; Pronoun.

Analysis:

- The alliterative "p" and joyous associations of "positive pleasure" emphasise the scale of bliss the animals feel, and the apparent success of Animalism.
- The repetition of "themselves", as well as the collective nature of the pronoun, highlights the new found independence the animals have achieved.
- The image of a "grudging master" foreshadows the horrors to come. Whilst Jones was "grudging", at least he fed the animals; on Animal Farm, by the end of the novel the animals are usually "hungry".

Use in essays on…Class; Hope; Pride; Truth; Responsibility.

Chapter Three:
"Nobody stole, nobody grumbled over his rations, the quarrelling and biting and jealousy which had been normal features of life in the old days had almost disappeared."

Interpretation: Animalism seems to bring social justice; equality for all animals is clear to see. However, tension and corruption are still evident.

Techniques: Tri-colon; Polysyndeton (repetition of 'and'); Tone.

Analysis:

- The polysyndeton in "quarrelling and biting and jealousy" emphasises the length of the animals' previous suffering under Jones.
- The tri-colon suggests earlier suffering was overwhelming – it was verbal ("quarrelling"), physical ("biting") and mental ("jealousy").
- Whilst seemingly perfect, there is an undertone of tension – "rations" suggests food is not plentiful, "almost disappeared" implies a threat remains, and all the suffering in the tri-colon comes from animal behaviour, not human.

Use in essays on… Class; Violence; Hope; Responsibility.

Chapter Three:
" "Comrades!" he cried. "You do not imagine, I hope, that we pigs are doing this in a spirit of selfishness and privilege?" "

Interpretation: Class differences are beginning to emerge between the animals, mainly due to the varying levels of intelligence, understanding and power.

Techniques: Pronoun; Sibilance; Sentence Structure; Tone.

Analysis:

- Whilst "Comrades" depicts the collective purpose of the animals and Animalism, the pronouns "you" and "we pigs" highlights a growing divide.
- The sibilance of "spirit of selfishness" accentuates the irony of the comment – the acts of drinking the milk and eating the apples were entirely selfish.
- The animals' ignorance is shown in the fact they fall for Squealer's use of rhetorical questions and manipulation – however, the sentence structure stresses "I hope", which could be seen as conveying a physical threat.

Use in essays on… Truth; Power; Class; Corruption; Ignorance.

Chapter Four:
"They were gored, kicked, bitten, trampled on. There was not an animal on the farm that did not take vengeance on them after his own fashion."

Interpretation: The vengeance and actions of the animals are understandable, and they defend Major's vision, but their violent behaviour still seems unsettling to the reader.

Techniques: Asyndeton; Language.

Analysis:
- The asyndetic list reminds the reader of the brutal, animalistic nature of all involved. Whilst Jones mistreated them, the animals have responded with a naturally wild, untamed instinct.
- "Take vengeance" gives a moral justification for the animals' actions and rebellion – they are dispensing justice for previous wrongs against them.
- The fact each animal took revenge "after his own fashion" stresses the importance of every animal as an individual and the liberation the farm could bring – each animal exerts their own actions in a free, unrestricted manner.

Use in essays on…Power; Class; Violence; Pride; Responsibility.

Chapter Four:
" "No sentimentality, comrade!" cried Snowball, from whose wounds the blood was still dripping. "War is war. The only good human being is a dead one." "

Interpretation: The ideals of rebellion and Animalism are still evident, as are Major's original words, but idealistic, justifiable revolution is turning into "war".

Techniques: Imagery; Repetition; Sentence Structure; Language.

Analysis:

- The physical imagery of "wounds" and "blood…dripping" suggest political change is only achieved through violent acts, as well as depicting Snowball's bravery on the battlefield.
- However, the repetition in "war is war", and the single clause sentence, depict a narrow, closed view of how to create change in the world.
- "Only" and "dead" are absolutes – it shows an inability to see any other ways of achieving peace and liberty.

Use in essays on…Power; Corruption; Violence; Ignorance; Pride; Truth.

Chapter Five:

"A publican, was stroking her nose and feeding her with sugar. Her coat was newly clipped and she wore a scarlet ribbon round her forelock. She appeared to be enjoying herself."

Interpretation: Mollie's apparently happy lifestyle working for Man is a direct threat to the essence of Animalism. Man is treating her well and she is thriving.

Techniques: Verbs; Language.

Analysis:

- The relationship between man and animal seems to be a loving one – the verb "stroking" is tender and friendly, and whilst Mollie relies on man for food, she is given "sugar", with its associations of treats and sweetness.
- Mollie's benefit is not just physical wellbeing. "Scarlet ribbon" and "newly clipped" imply care and attention has been lavished upon her.
- "Enjoying herself" suggests that as well as her physical wellbeing, Mollie's mindset is one of contentment, unlike those who remain on the farm.

Use in essays on…Pride; Truth; Ignorance; Hope; Responsibility.

Chapter Five:

Interpretation: Like Major, Snowball is convincing in his speeches and his use of rhetoric, but we learn that violence and corruption will always defeat idealised words.

Techniques: Alliteration; Verbs; Adjectives.

Analysis:

- Alliteration stresses "painted" and "picture" – neither convey a factual depiction of the future. Both imply imagination and an idealised vision, not truth. "Glowing" implies a beacon of light, but it is not the truth.
- "When" and "was" indicate a certainty to the future Snowball describes, yet "might be" implies Snowball's ideas will not definitely be achieved.
- It is not "labour" that is the issue – the adjective "sordid" stresses it is the dirty, demeaning nature of the work that is the problem.

Use in essays on…Pride; Hope; Power; Ignorance; Violence; Truth; Class.

Chapter Five:
"Squealer spoke so persuasively, and the three dogs who happened to be with him growled so threateningly, that they accepted his explanation without further questions."

Interpretation: The abandonment of the 7th Commandment ("All animals are equal") is clear. Equality has been replaced with the violent oppression of dictatorship.

Techniques: Adverbs; Juxtaposition; Alliteration.

Analysis:

- The adverbs emphasise two conflicting ways of maintaining political control — "persuasively" implies seeking collective agreement, juxtaposed with "threateningly", which suggests leadership and control through fear.
- This is enhanced by Squealer's actions — the alliterative "Squealer spoke" implies reasonable dialogue, juxtaposed with the violent oppression of "growled".
- "Accepted" is not a sign of agreement between equals — it is an abuse of power, the oppression of the ignorant through corrupt and violent means.

Use in essays on…Power; Corruption; Ignorance; Violence; Truth.

Chapter Six:

"One Sunday morning, when the animals assembled to receive their orders, Napoleon announced that he had decided upon a new policy."

Interpretation: Sunday, a traditional day of rest, resembles a military scene where a dictator demands his people conform. It is the very opposite of Major's vision.

Techniques: Language; Alliteration; Juxtaposition.

Analysis:

- The nouns "orders" and "policy" as well as the verbs "decided" and "announced" all accentuate the growing dictatorship of Napoleon.
- This is reinforced by the associations of the passive action "receive" – the animals clearly have no role in decision-making on the farm.
- The alliterative "animals assembled" is an image of collective oppression and loss of individuality, juxtaposed with the independence of the singular "he had". Society on the farm is now structured around a hierarchy of power.

Use in essays on… Power; Class; Corruption; Ignorance; Responsibility.

 "It was also more suited to the dignity of the Leader (for of late he had taken to speaking of Napoleon under the title of 'Leader') to live in a house than in a mere sty."

Interpretation: Different classes and hierarchies are clearly developing on the farm, and the 7th Commandment is eroded even further as Napoleon becomes more human.

Techniques: Irony; Proper Nouns; Language; Tone.

Analysis:

- The noun "dignity" is highly ironic – as Napoleon apparently becomes more dignified, the farm animals are degraded even further.
- This idea is developed with the use of the adjective "mere", the tone of which is incredibly dismissive of the life the animals lead.
- Much like the animals have had their individual identities removed on the farm, so too has Napoleon – however, he is now defined by rank, with the regal, powerful proper noun of "Leader" creating even greater hierarchy on the farm.

Use in essays on…Power; Class; Corruption; Pride; Truth.

Chapter Seven:
"It was a bitter winter. The stormy weather was followed by sleet and snow, and then by a hard frost which did not break till well into February."

Interpretation: Both Major and Snowball depicted a future where animals would be working and interacting harmoniously with nature – here the reality is far bleaker.

Techniques: Pathetic Fallacy; Adjectives; Sibilance; Imagery.

Analysis:

- The pathetic fallacy mimics the life of the animals – "stormy" represents the tension on the farm, and "hard frost" accentuates the physical hardship they endure.
- The image of a "bitter winter" conveys a biting coldness – the reader is unsure who will "break" first, the animals or the season.
- The sibilant "s" in "sleet and snow" creates a continuous sound, mimicking the weather's constant assault upon the animals.

Use in essays on…Hope; Truth; Responsibility.

"They were all slain on the spot. And so the tale of confessions and executions went on, until there was a pile of corpses lying before Napoleon's feet and the air was heavy with the smell of blood."

Interpretation: Napoleon's actions are swift and brutal, designed to create fear and compliance amongst the farm animals. It closely mirrors Stalin's Purges in 1930s Russia.

Techniques: Sibilance; Imagery; Language.

Analysis:

- The sibilance of "slain on the spot" emphasises the swiftness, terror and brutality of Napoleon's actions, far worse than anything Jones used to do.
- "Confessions" is ironic as they are not true confessions – the reader sees a further erosion of truth in favour of rhetoric.
- The auditory (hearing "confessions"), visual ("pile of corpses"), and physical ("heavy" air) nature of the scene, as well as the "smell of blood", overwhelms the senses and emphasises the utter failure to achieve the freedom they desired.

Use in essays on… Power; Corruption; Violence.

Chapter Seven:

> "The hayfield, the spinney, the drinking pool, the ploughed fields where the young wheat was thick and green, and the red roofs of the farm buildings with the smoke curling from the chimney."

Interpretation: The farm itself is a natural, beautiful place, comfortably able to provide for all animals. It is those who have power on the farm that end up corrupting it.

Techniques: Asyndeton; Language; Imagery; Alliteration.

Analysis:

- The asyndetic list stresses the fact the farm could provide for all their needs – "hayfield" (for bedding), "spinney" (for shelter), "drinking pool" (for water) and "ploughed fields" (for food) covers all their animalistic needs.
- "Young wheat" alludes to potential, growth and plenty – it was unfortunately a dream that never happened.
- "Thick and green" implies a natural abundance of food, and the colours "green" and the alliterative "red roofs" highlights the beauty the farm could achieve.

Use in essays on… Corruption; Hope; Pride; Truth.

Chapter Eight:
"Boxer put out his nose to sniff at the bank-notes, and the flimsy white things stirred and rustled in his breath."

Interpretation: Napoleon takes great pride in his money, but money is a human creation. Animals do not need it – it brings nothing but social unrest and corruption.

Techniques: Language; Verbs; Adjectives.

Analysis:

- Boxer, a symbol of integrity and morality, does nothing but "sniff" at the money, suggesting a great distrust and distaste for the bank notes.
- The fragile associations of the verbs "stirred" and "rustled" highlight the vulnerability of the animals – one breath and it could all be gone.
- The adjective "flimsy" implies the value of money is questionable, accentuated by the vague noun "things", suggesting money has no real value.

Use in essays on…Class; Corruption; Ignorance; Responsibility.

Chapter Eight:

Interpretation: The pigs' corruption is plain to see to the reader; they have taken on the worst excesses of mankind and have come full circle.

Techniques: Alliteration; Language; Symbolism.

Analysis:

- The verb "sprawling" alongside "overturned" both signify that the farm is falling apart in an uncontrolled, dangerous manner.
- The alliterative "lay a lantern" alludes to the fact a light needs to be shed on the pigs' behaviour, but it is swiftly hidden from view.
- Furthermore, the alliterative "ring round" symbolises the secrecy that has engulfed the farm – "round" suggests the pigs' behaviour is concealed by an unbreakable "ring".

Use in essays on… Truth; Corruption; Ignorance; Responsibility.

Chapter Nine:
"Young pigs were given their instruction by Napoleon himself in the farmhouse kitchen. They took their exercise in the garden, and were discouraged from playing with the other young animals."

Interpretation: Having defeated Snowball and taken over the farm, Napoleon now seeks to remove all innocence from the young pigs and make them his loyal followers.

Techniques: Repetition; Setting; Juxtaposition.

Analysis:

- The repetition of "young" stresses the corruption and indoctrination of innocence by the political establishment, much like in Stalinist Russia.
- Major wanted all animals to be free and to avoid man's tyranny – Napoleon now exists in the most domestic and human of settings, the "farmhouse kitchen", and dictates "instruction".
- The military associations of "exercise" juxtapose with the gentle, idyllic and natural associations of "garden".

Use in essays on…Power; Corruption; Innocence.

Chapter Nine:
" "Fools! Fools!" shouted Benjamin, prancing round them and stamping the earth with his small hoofs. "Fools! Do you not see what is written on the side of that van?" "

Interpretation: Benjamin's ability to see the truth is essentially futile – he is aware of what is happening on the farm but cannot stop it.

Techniques: Language; Repetition.

Analysis:

- Whilst many of the animals are unintelligent, the repetition of "fools" places blame on them for their ignorance – they are naïve and unaware of the horrors around them, too often blindly accepting what they are told.
- Benjamin is angry for the first time, but his powerlessness is emphasised by "shouted", "prancing" and "stamping" – he is unable to stop the pigs.
- "Small hoofs" are a symbol of Benjamin's helplessness. He has no power or authority; "do you not see" stresses that even though he has the intelligence to "see" the truth, he cannot change the course of events.

Use in essays on…Power; Ignorance; Truth.

Chapter Ten:
"The farm possessed three horses now besides Clover. They were fine upstanding beasts, willing workers and good comrades, but very stupid."

Interpretation: The farm has reverted to the way it was under Jones' ownership. It is not the utopia Major dreamed of, but rather a farm designed to make profit.

Techniques: Alliteration; Tri-colon; Language.

Analysis:

- The adverb "very" is key – the horses' stupidity, their inability to question or challenge authority, is vital to the success of Napoleon's plan.
- The verb "possessed" implies these horses are not free, but rather owned by the farm as property.
- The tri-colon emphasises animals are not part of a society, but part of a work force – "upstanding beasts" suggests physically capable, "good comrade" implies they are compliant, and the alliterative "willing worker" stresses their dedication to the cause at hand without question.

Use in essays on…Corruption; Class; Ignorance.

"Things never had been, nor ever could be, much better or much worse – hunger, hardship and disappointment being, so he said, the unalterable law of life."

Interpretation: Old Benjamin's views juxtapose those of Major as he approached the end of his life. Rather than offer defiant hope, he gives nothing more than resigned truth.

Techniques: Tri-colon; Alliteration; Repetition.

Analysis:

- The tri-colon emphasises the variety of suffering faced – the alliterative "hunger, hardship" depicts physical suffering, made worse by the mental suffering of "disappointment".
- The alliteration in "law of life" highlights the rigidity of an animal's existence – pain is "unalterable" and "inevitable."
- An animal's life is essentially hopeless – the repetition of "much" alongside "never" implies life will always be entirely mundane, never experiencing "much better".

Use in essays on…Hope; Pride; Truth.

Chapter Ten:
"Twelves voices were shouting in anger, and they were all alike. No question, now, what had happened to the faces of the pigs. The creatures outside looked from pig to man, and from man to pig, and from pig to man again."

Interpretation: Just as Man was depicted as animal-like at the start of the novel, the pigs have now become like Man – power has eventually corrupted all.

Techniques: Personification; Repetition; Alliteration.

Analysis:

- The personification of pigs "shouting in anger" completes the transformation – the pigs have become human.
- The repetition of "pig to man", "man to pig" and "pig to man again" depicts the interchangeable nature of man and animal – they are now one and the same.
- The alliteration of "all alike" and collective nature of the pronoun "all" confirm the original vision for Animal Farm is now dead.

Use in essays on… Power; Corruption; Violence; Responsibility.

Major Themes

Corruption	Ignorance	Responsibility
Power	Class	Truth
Violence	Hope	Pride

Major Characters

Napoleon	Snowball	Squealer
Boxer	Mollie	Benjamin
Major	Mr Jones	The Dogs

One mistake people often make is to try to revise EVERYTHING!

This is clearly not possible.

Instead, once you know and understand the plot, a great idea is to pick three or four major themes, and three or four major characters, and revise these in great detail.

If, for example, you revised Corruption and Power, you will also have covered a huge amount of material to use in questions about Napoleon, Squealer or Class.

Or, if you revised Responsibility and Mr Jones, you would certainly have plenty of material if a question on Violence, Hope or Boxer was set.

Use the following framework as a basis for setting *any* of your own revision questions – simply swap the theme or character to create a new essay title!

How does Orwell portray the theme of __________ in *Animal Farm*?

How does the character of __________ develop as the novel progresses?

How does Orwell explore truth in Animal Farm?

Much like Major's earlier call to action, Snowball sounds convincing in his speeches and his use of rhetoric, but the reader learns that violence and corruption will always defeat idealised words. Whilst the animals believe Snowball's "glowing sentences", with "glowing" suggesting a beacon of light and truth, Orwell's use of alliteration stresses "painted" and "picture" – neither convey a factual depiction of the future (both imply imagination, not truth), and create an idealised vision. It is beautiful, but not achievable. Furthermore, "when" and "was" indicate a certainty to the future Snowball describes, yet "might be" implies Snowball's ideas will not definitely be achieved. Snowball is also blind to the true motivation behind some animals' behaviour. Snowball believes it is not "labour" that is the issue for animals; instead, the adjective "sordid" stresses it is the dirty, demeaning nature of the work that is the problem. Whilst most animals share Snowball's willingness to work as long as the "labour" is dignified, he doesn't see the truth in Napoleon's character – Napoleon is willing to abuse those around him so that he does not need to work, "sordid" or not.

Potential Essay Questions

How is Napoleon portrayed in *Animal Farm*?

Topic Sentence 1: Napoleon is strong, powerful and controlling – a dictator, not a leader of equals.

Use: Pages 21 and 27.

Topic Sentence 2: Much of his power comes from his ability to utilise his deputies and remove non-conformers.

Use: Pages 16 and 23.

Topic Sentence 3: Benjamin sees through him, but is powerless to act.

Use: Pages 28 and 30.

Topic Sentence 4: Ultimately, Napoleon corrupts Animalism to suit his own needs.

Use: Pages 11 and 31.

Topic Sentence 1: A social system based around equality should be possible as the farm environment is able to supply the needs of all animals equally and fairly.

Use: Pages 10 and 12.

Topic Sentence 2: For an equal, classless society to exist, rules need to be put in place to secure fair treatment for all.

Use: Pages 11 and 13.

Topic Sentence 3: However, differences in intellectual ability mean equality can be manipulated to give power and status to those willing to take it.

Use: Pages 18 and 19.

Topic Sentence 4: In a society that needs rules, laws and order to function, a leader will always emerge, and a system of class and hierarchy will overthrow equality.

Use: Pages 20 and 21.

Topic Sentence 1: The farm is a place of natural beauty, an environment that provides food, water and leisure, and could certainly fulfil Major's dream.

Use: Pages 10 and 12.

Topic Sentence 2: The farm contained instruments of oppression in Jones' reign, but once they are removed it has the potential to be an idealised, natural home.

Use: Pages 9 and 24.

Topic Sentence 3: However, the natural world is frequently harsh and unforgiving – the world outside the farm, controlled by humans, could be seen as safer.

Use: Pages 17 and 22.

Topic Sentence 4: The farm itself becomes corrupted, tainted by the pursuit of money and other unnatural elements.

Use: Pages 25 and 29.

Topic Sentence 1: The power to control one's own life and be in charge of one's own destiny is the driving force behind the rebellion and of Animalism.

Use: Pages 7 and 8.

Topic Sentence 2: Despite this idealised concept, power is often only achievable through the use of violence.

Use: Pages 15 and 26.

Topic Sentence 3: Yet Orwell also suggests the key to maintaining power and control over others is through intelligence and manipulation.

Use: Pages 14 and 19.

Topic Sentence 4: However power is gained, and whatever purpose it is meant to serve, it will always lead to corruption.

Use: Pages 26 and 31.

Major characters and themes – Take any of the major characters and themes (see page 32 for a list) and group together quotations in sets of 2 or 3 to answer the following question: "How does the theme/character develop as the novel goes on?"

You should try to get 4 sets of quotations, giving you 8-12 overall.

A great cover and repeat exercise – Cover the whole page, apart from the quotation at the top. Can you now fill in the four sections in your exercise book without looking – Interpretations, Techniques, Analysis, Use in essays on…?

This also works really well as a revision activity with a friend – cover the whole card, apart from the quotation at the top. If you read out the quotation, can they tell you the four sections without looking – Interpretations, Techniques, Analysis, Use in essays on…?

"The Development Game" – Pick any quotation at random from The Quotation Bank and use it to create an essay question, and then create a focused topic sentence to start the essay. Next, find another appropriate quotation to develop your idea even further.

"The Contrast Game" – Follow the same rules as The Development Game, but instead of finding a quotation to support your idea, find a quotation that can be used to start a counter-argument.

Your very own Quotation Bank! Using the same headings and format as The Quotation Bank, find 10 more quotations from throughout the text (select them from many different sections of the text to help develop whole text knowledge) and create your own revision cards.

Essay writing – They aren't always fun, but writing essays is great revision. Choose a practice question and then try taking three quotations and writing out a perfect paragraph, making sure you add connectives, technical vocabulary and sophisticated language.

Glossary

Alliteration – Repetition of the same consonant or sound at the beginning of a number of words in a sentence to create emphasis: "crystal clear" emphasises the clarity and purity of Major's vision.

Allusion – Referring to something in a sentence without mentioning it explicitly: "Commandments" has deeply biblical allusions, implying the laws have a religious truth to them.

Asyndeton – The omission of conjunctions within a sentence: "gored, kicked, bitten, trampled on" reminds the reader of the brutal, animalistic nature of all involved.

Imagery – Figurative language that appeals to the senses of the audience: imagery of "dew", "summer grass" and "black earth" depict nature as it should be enjoyed.

Irony – A statement that suggests one thing but often has a contrary meaning: "dignity" is highly ironic – as Napoleon apparently becomes more dignified, the farm animals are degraded even further.

Juxtaposition – Two ideas, images or words placed next to each other to create a contrasting effect: "persuasively" implies seeking collective agreement, juxtaposed with "threateningly", which suggests leadership and control through fear.

Language – The vocabulary chosen to create effect.

Pathetic Fallacy – The weather or environment mimics the mood or actions of the novel to enhance the effect: "stormy" represents the tension on the farm, and "hard frost" accentuates the physical hardship they endure.

Personification – A non-human object or concept takes on human qualities to make its presence more vivid to the audience: the violent "knives" are personified as "cruel", suggesting an even darker element of evil control to Mr Jones' previous behaviour.

Polysyndeton – The repetition of conjunctions such as "and" one after another: "quarrelling and biting and jealousy" lengthens the scale of the animals' previous suffering.

Repetition – When a word, phrase or idea is repeated to reinforce it: the repetition of "fools" places blame on the animals for their ignorance at Boxer's death.

Sentence Structure – The way the writer has ordered the words in a sentence to create a certain effect: in Squealer's speech, the sentence structure stresses "I hope", which could be seen as conveying a physical threat.

Sibilance – A variation on alliteration, usually of the 's' sound, that creates a hissing sound: the sibilance of "slain on the spot" emphasises the swiftness, terror and brutality of Napoleon's actions, far worse than anything Jones used to do.

Symbolism – The use of a symbol to represent an idea: "ring round" symbolises the secrecy that has engulfed the farm – "round" suggests the pigs' behaviour is concealed by an unbreakable "ring".

Tri-colon – A list of three words or phrases for effect: "upstanding beasts" suggests physically capable, "good comrade" implies they are compliant, and the alliterative "willing worker" stresses their dedication to the cause at hand without question.